Discover Series
LAGARTIJAS

Lagartija Monitor Argus

Dragón Barbudo

Lagartija Moteada Marrón

Lagartija Rayado Marrón

Camaleón

Lagartija de Pincel

Cameleón Pantera

Gecko Crestado

Broche Brillante de Lagartija

Lagartija de Cuello Volante

Gecko

Monstruo Gila

Iguana Verde

Dragón de Agua Indio

Newt Warty de Laos

Gecko Leopardo

Lagartija Monitor

Camaleón Pantera

Lagartija Monitor de Garganta Durazno

Salamandra

Dragón Barbudo de Espalda de Seda sin Escamas

Gecko Tokay

Camaleón Joven

Make Sure to Check Out the Other Discover Series Books from Xist Publishing:

Published in the United States by Xist Publishing
www.xistpublishing.com
PO Box 61593 Irvine, CA 92602

© 2018 by Xist Publishing All rights reserved
Translated by Victor Santana
No portion of this book may be reproduced without express permission of the publisher
All images licensed from Fotolia
First Bilingual Edition

ISBN: 978-1-5324-0719-2   eISBN: 978-1-5324-0720-8

xist Publishing

www.ingramcontent.com/pod-product-compliance
Lightning Source LLC
LaVergne TN
LVHW070950070426
835507LV00030B/3484